To Becky,

lifted by *You*

a heart changed by perfect love

So thrilled to include your heart image
in this book... Such a beautiful and
Cherished gift from our Heavenly Father.
Thanks for sharing the love! May God

CONNIE SMITH

bless you always. Love you much!

Connie Smith

Lifted by You: A Heart Changed by Perfect Love

Text and photographs copyright © 2017 by Connie Smith

First Edition: November 2017

ISBN: 978-0-9906651-3-7

Library of Congress Control Number: 2017910362

1. Inspiration 2. Hope 3. Encouragement 4. Love 5. Spirituality 6. Faith
I. Smith, Connie II. Lifted by You

Lifted by You may be purchased at special quantity discounts for sales promotions, premiums, corporate programs, gifts, and fundraising. For pricing information or to have Connie speak at your event, call 615-496-7006 or send an email to connie@neverloseheart.com.

Scriptures taken from the Holy Bible, New International Version®, NIV®. Copyright © 1973, 1978, 1984, 2011 by Biblica, Inc.™ Used by permission of Zondervan. All rights reserved worldwide. www.zondervan.com The "NIV" and "New International Version" are trademarks registered in the United States Patent and Trademark Office by Biblica, Inc.™

Editor: Dave Carew
Designer: Cheryl Casey
Author Photograph: Todd Adams
Publisher: Never Lose Heart LLC

Printed in China.

www.neverloseheart.com
www.facebook.com/neverloseheartbook
www.instagram.com/neverloseheartbook

Because Your love
is better than life, my lips will glorify You.

Psalm 63:3

Dedication

As I write this, it's Father's Day. The first Father's Day since my dad passed away on December 20, 2016. I am overwhelmed by the steadfast love of my Heavenly Father and the realization of how it has filled me, changed me, sustained me, healed me, and lifted me. And I am overwhelmed by the immense love I feel today for my earthly father, whom I was not close to, as I imagine him in Heaven, fully healed and restored, waiting to see me again. I look forward to his embrace and to that new day when we can start over, fearlessly building the relationship I know he always wanted with me deep within, just as much as I wanted it with him. I am overwhelmed by this miracle in my heart and filled with gratitude for how God has used everything in my journey to lead me to this place. It is with this heart that I dedicate *Lifted by You: A Heart Changed by Perfect Love* to my dad.

acknowledgments

One of the greatest joys that has come from publishing my books is to see how you, my friends/readers, have been inspired to see God's love all around you. Every time I receive an email or a text message with a heart image, it warms my heart, especially when there is a story behind it or when God has used it to speak to you in a specific way. These love letters from God are such gifts to be cherished, so thank you to those who have taken the time to share your encounters. As a way of showcasing this movement, I have chosen to feature some of these photos in this book, in addition to my own photos. Thank you to the following people for graciously allowing me to include yours:

Nevaeh Baker (page 102); Andrew Brock (page 61); Bobbie Jo Carver (pages 17 and 57); Jessica Clemons (page 110); Cindy Comperry (page 77); Lily and Jeff Culbreath (page 81); Pamela Daugherty (page 93); Beth Easter (pages 41, 49, and 105); Ruth Elliott (page 54); John Fletcher (page 94); Karen Gonzales (page 114); Leslie Henderson (page 121); Judy Hoosier (page 70); Grace Ahn Hundley (page 98); Adriane Ketelsen (page 46); Becky Kown (page 53); Sandra Ledbetter (page 89); Melissa Linscott (page 97); Molly Neu (page 42); Laura O'Shoney (page 18); Brenda Roggy (pages 73 and 125); Helen Rolf (page 29); Melissa Russell (page 65); Lora Schrock (page 122); Hudson Speece (page 22); Samantha Star (page 74); Jenny Stock (page 106); Zee Stokes (page 133); Heidi Tieslau (page 30); Rachel Wachtel (pages 34, 50, 109, and 130); Drew Weresuk (page 82); Sharon West (page 17); Mary Glynn Williamson (page 26).

Heartfelt gratitude to my dear friends and family who helped me bring this book to completion, including Todd Adams, Allen Baun, Amy Biter, Dave Carew, Cheryl Casey, Cindy Comperry, Lily Culbreath (sister), Anne Kufeldt, Peggy Schaefer, Billie Ann Smith (mom), Marshall Smith (brother), Jenny Stock, and Tim Weaver. I love you all!

An extra thank you to my mom for tirelessly praying for me and for inspiring me with your unshakable faith and huge heart of love, and to my sister for all the ways you encourage and support me.

preface

We have all lived in the shadows at some point. And many of us who have come out of the shadows still find ourselves slipping back into darkness and gloom. Some of us have stayed there for so long that we've become comfortable there. We have believed the lie that God is not who He says He is, or we can't get past the devastations or disappointments in our lives. If God is love, or if God is "for us," then why did He allow this or that? Or, perhaps we believe we can't measure up to His standards because we think that's what a successful relationship with Him is all about. So, forget it. And we decide to stay where we are and not let God in. Because it just seems easier that way.

The voice of doubt will always try to get the best of us, intending to rob us of everything that God, in His amazing love, went to great lengths to secure for us. When I stop and think about what He has done for you and for me through His one and only son, Jesus, it brings tears to my eyes. Not only did the ruler of the universe come to this earth in human likeness to die in our place, setting us free from the law of sin and death so that we could live eternally with Him, but He suffered immense rejection and crucifixion on a cross, of all things—the lowest, most humiliating, shameful, and painful form of death in the ancient world.

If He went through all of that for us, why would He fail us now? He redeemed us not so that we can wander in the darkness and live defeated lives. He redeemed us so that we can rise above the power of darkness and live the purposeful life He designed for us. He died with outstretched arms. What a picture of His amazing love toward us. The hands that were nailed to that cross reach toward us today with infinite love to heal and to liberate.

So why do many of us find ourselves unable to conquer the shadows of despair or rise above old, destructive patterns? Is this you? What keeps you there? If it's not that you have lost hope, could it be that you are so wrapped up in picking up the pieces from a broken past, and trying to fix yourself, that you are stifling the power of God's love—the love that will mend you and begin making you whole?

I have been there.

It took going down a long, desolate road—where I became so exhausted from trying to be a "better person" in order to gain God's approval— that, eventually, I gave up. I had nothing left to give but a worn-out, broken heart. If God was real and would take me as I am, I needed to know it.

Little did I know how powerful that simple, yet honest, cry from my heart would be in setting me on a path to have a true encounter with God's love. That is when I began seeing hearts *everywhere*. My heart became overwhelmed as I began to see myself through the eyes of my Heavenly Father and understand the true meaning of His grace. As I began to rest in the assurance of His unconditional love, it not only filled me, but it began to transform and empower me. I was able to forgive those who had hurt me, accept myself, and ultimately break the chains of darkness in my life. His perfect love has brought true healing to my heart. I am still a work in progress, as new layers continue to be uncovered, but there's hope and peace in every step of the journey.

I believe that God longs to make Himself known to all of us in a real way. He desires that we know His unfailing love intimately and deeply—not just in our heads, but deep within our hearts—so that we will fully trust Him. It's the place where true and lasting change begins. It is the foundation that allows us to confidently walk our journey to wholeness. It is the fuel that heals us, and the power that drives out the darkness.

There is more to this life than trying to make it through the day. Don't let the shadows of life rob you of joy or hope…or keep you in destructive patterns…or prevent you from fulfilling God's divine purposes for your life. In God's amazing grace there is power to rise above—if we choose to open our hearts and believe.

introduction

Third in the Never Lose Heart book series, *Lifted by You: A Heart Changed by Perfect Love,* is written as a response to the first two books, *Never Lose Heart* and *Grounded in His Love* which are intended to be read as love letters from God. This book is what I have come to know about God's love at the core of my heart on the other side of challenges. And it's the response and attitude I *want* to live out each and every day when new challenges come my way. However, I am quick to admit that I can still be slow to come around. Because let's face it, we are human, and we tend to want what we want when we want it. Instant answers. Instant resolutions. Instant remedies. Trusting God and waiting on Him is easier said than done sometimes.

My prayer is that *Lifted by You* will remind us that God *always* has our best interest in mind and that this book will inspire us to look more on the side of hope, no matter what situations we encounter. Because there is always hope. God is always working on our behalf, leading us deeper in our walk with Him, so that we can go higher. Every challenge, heartache, and disappointment presents us with an opportunity to lean in closer, and ultimately, to see His good purposes.

When we fall, may we quickly get back up, believing, trusting, and persevering in the One who paid it all, so that we might live our lives nothing short of victorious. We can rest assured that His amazing grace is sufficient and will continue to mature us until He takes us home.

Where can I go that You
will not be with me?

If I climb toward the heavens,
You are there.

If I make my bed in the valley,
You are there.

Your relentless love
knows no boundaries.

Your faithfulness reaches
to the skies.

I am overwhelmed by Your
beauty and all that You are.

When my life turns upside down,

I will look to You…

because Your peace refreshes
the depths of my soul.

When I encounter setbacks on
my journey, I will praise You…

because You will not let
my failures and hardships
go to waste.

When I receive a bad report,
I will rest in You…

because You cover me in the shadow of Your almighty wings.

When I am pierced by the
darkness, I will lean on You…

because You give me the
power to rise above.

When You take me through fires
of testing, I will abide in You…

because You refine me like gold,
making me more like You.

When You don't answer
according to my prayers,
I will yield to You…

because You are for me, and
Your ways are higher than mine.

When You call me to step
outside my comfort zone,
I will serve You...

because You are with me, and
You prepare the way before me.

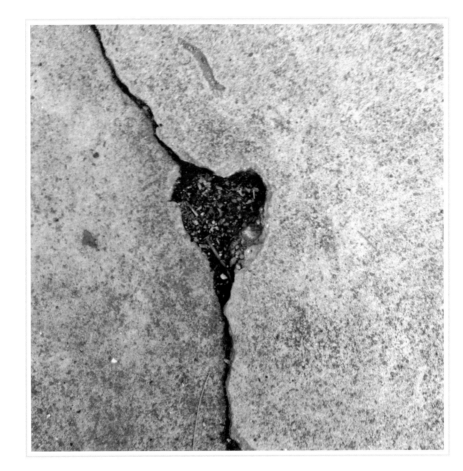

When fear and anxiety creep in,

I will call out to You…

because Your name is a
strong tower, a place of
refuge in the storm.

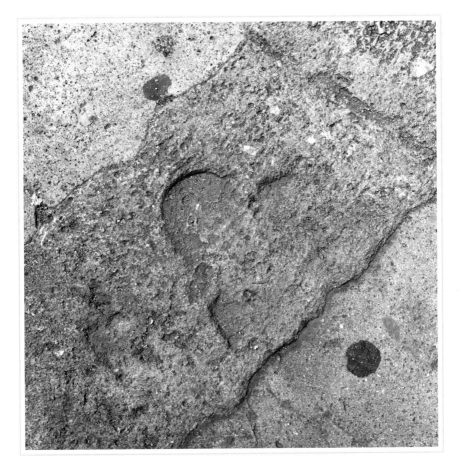

When I need concrete advice
or wisdom, I will seek You…

because Your word is a
light for my path.

When I discover holes in my heart, I will kneel before You…

because You heal and restore,
one layer at a time.

When I feel condemned
and torn apart,
I will remember You…

because Your grace has
already washed me clean.

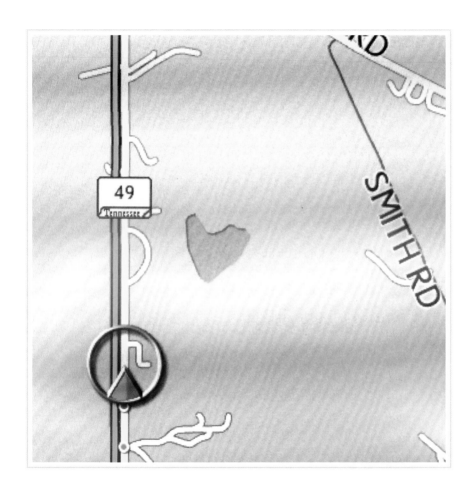

When I feel hurt or offended, I will take the high road and forgive...

because Your mercies for me
are new every morning.

When prickly people cross my path, I will choose to love…

because You see all my flaws
and love me unconditionally.

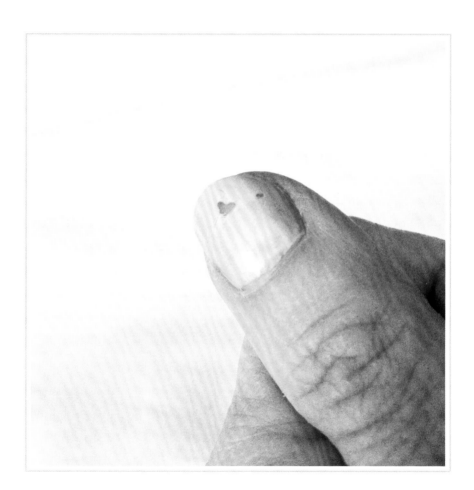

When I feel pressured
by the world around me,
I will follow You…

because You loved me first
with a love so deep.

When I feel the weight of grief and sorrow, I will worship You…

because in Your presence
there is fullness of joy.

When I feel distant from You,

I will persevere in You...

because Your love is wrapped
around me, even when
I don't feel it.

When the waiting seems
stretched beyond reason,
I will submit to You…

because You see how
each thread is woven into
Your beautiful design.

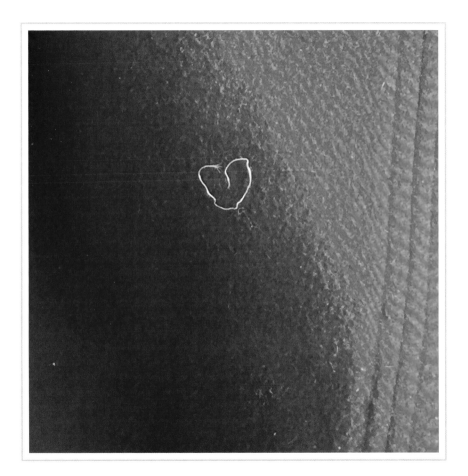

When the writing is on the wall,

I will thank You…

because Your new beginnings
spring forth after winter.

When a door closes and leaves
me in the cold, I will trust You…

because You have a
purposeful plan and will
lead me, step by step.

When I feel brushed
over or forgotten,
I will draw near to You…

because You raise me
up in due time.

When the chips are down,

I will rely on You…

because You are all-powerful
and supply all my needs.

When I am touched by
goodness and love,
I will sing Your praises…

because every good and
perfect gift is from You.

When I fail You or don't love
You with my whole heart…

please envelop me with the
light of Your love…

that I might have eyes to see
how I break Your heart…

and have the humility to
surrender once again.

Your love makes me strong.

Your love makes me brave.

The more I am grounded in You…

the more I am lifted up…

soaring in Your spirit…

and shining with Your glory.

Because of Your great love…

I will never lose heart.

lifted by *You*

"Because of the Lord's great love we are not consumed, for his compassions never fail. They are new every morning; great is your faithfulness."

Lamentations 3:22-23

about the author

Connie Smith grew up in Nashville, Tennessee. She graduated from the University of Tennessee in 1994 with a degree in Marketing and has spent most of her professional career in Nashville in the healthcare and publishing industries. After resigning as an executive in 2009 to pursue a business venture that did not unfold as she had hoped, she suddenly found herself in a desolate place. In part, this began a quest to connect with God in a deeper way and, ultimately, to find her purpose. Little did she know the journey itself would produce the elements for a project she would later discover to be her sought-after passion. *Never Lose Heart* was born out of this journey in 2014 and marked her debut as an inspirational writer. Two years later, she published *Grounded in His Love* followed by *Lifted by You*. In addition to her love for writing, Connie enjoys spending time with family and friends, leading Bible study discussion groups at her home, cooking and entertaining, art, hiking, nature, and being outdoors.

other books

Never Lose Heart series

To view a portion of these books and check out other
Never Lose Heart products, please visit www.neverloseheart.com.

share your photos

Have you seen a heart? We would love for you to share it with us! Please email your photo to connie@neverloseheart.com, along with your permission to include it in Never Lose Heart's Community Gallery at www.neverloseheart.com.

To receive information about book-signing events, special promotions, and new products/books, please sign up for our newsletter at www.neverloseheart.com. To book Connie as a speaker for your event, please contact her at connie@neverloseheart.com.

Follow us:

@neverloseheartbook